BASS BUILDERS

Audio
Access
Included

reggae bass

T0034040

by *Ed Friedland*

THE COMPLETE GUIDE TO REGGAE
AND JAMAICAN BASS STYLES

To access audio visit:
www.halleonard.com/mylibrary

Enter Code
2331-5173-9623-2469

ISBN 978-0-7935-7994-5

HAL•LEONARD®
CORPORATION

7777 W. BLUEMOUND RD. P.O. BOX 13819 MILWAUKEE, WI 53213

Visit Hal Leonard Online at
www.halleonard.com

CONTENTS

FOREWORD

Although small in size, the island of Jamaica is one of the most musically fertile places on earth. While her larger neighbor, Cuba, exerts a major influence in the world of jazz, Jamaica's infiltration and transformation of international pop music through Reggae (mostly dominated by American and British groups) is unprecedented for such a tiny, economically challenged country.

While musically related to other Caribbean styles like Trinidadian calypso and Haitian compas, Reggae retains its own unique style, and has been far more influential than any of its Afro-Caribbean cousins. The 1970s saw reggae (or reggae-influenced) songs being cut by pop stars like Paul Simon, Paul McCartney, the Rolling Stones, and Eric Clapton, yet by mid-decade, reggae was still considered "underground" enough to be appropriated by punk bands like The Clash and The Slits.

Reggae continues to have a huge influence on pop music across the world to this day. Consider these facts:

- The current ska craze is based (loosely) on a style of Jamaican music from the early 60s, although few fans of bands like Goldfinger or Reel Big Fish may realize it.

- The "techno" movement that spawned groups like Prodigy and Madonna's newest work is inspired in part by Jamaican *dub* music. Dub began as a novelty in the early seventies when producers started adding tape delay and other effects to the instrumental B-sides of popular singles.

- Most significantly, Rap music also has strong roots in Jamaica. In 1970 a DJ named U Roy made hit records by rapping over popular songs of a few years earlier. This style, called "chatting," "toasting," or just "DJ" in Jamaica has been hugely popular ever since. Jamaican immigrants eventually brought it to New York City in the 1970s, and the rest is history.

Reggae's remarkable influence and staying power is largely due to its fascinating history. Reggae's rich and varied cultural lineage combines the musical traditions of African slaves and the Europeans that took control of the island during its history. A later period of influence occurred in the second half of the twentieth century when jazz and R&B music came across the Caribbean on radio waves from stations in Miami and New Orleans. As well, sound system owners were buying up American "race" records such as Louis Jordan and Rosco Gordon to play at all-night dance parties, a common form of weekend entertainment for many Jamaicans. The sound system has long been the lifeblood of the Jamaican music industry. Wealthy Jamaicans and tourists could afford to go out and see live bands perform, but the poor people could only afford to hear music at the large mobile discotheques that were set up wherever there was enough space to dance and sell beer and food. Sound system owners like Clement "Coxsone" Dodd started out by bringing back R&B records from the USA, but when it became harder to find the sort of records that went over well in Jamaica, Dodd (along with most of his rivals) were soon recording their own records at home.

Though most of the early records were simple stylistic knock-offs of American songs, Jamaican musicians were soon expanding on them, adding their own flavor. The result was a uniquely danceable form of music called Ska, named after the sound the guitar made as it strummed on the "and" of every beat. When Jamaica won its independence from the UK in 1962, the government declared Ska the official music of young Jamaica. Developing it into a unique sound became a matter not only of music, but of patriotism! By the end of 1966, the beat had slowed down into a style known as *Rock Steady*, which, with its new emphasis on the electric bass, prefigured the Reggae music that was to develop by the end of the decade.

Throughout the development of Jamaican pop music, continuing up to the present day, the popularity of the sound systems has remained constant. Most classic Jamaican music—from the Wailers' first hit, "Simmer Down," to the latest cuts from Buju Banton or Beenie Man—has been produced not primarily for radio play or retail sale, but for the dancehall. A song isn't considered successful unless it inspires an enthusiastic response from a hot, sweaty room full of tired people. Reggae isn't music that encourages subtle experimentation, but neither does it tolerate self-indulgent pretensions.

In Jamaica, the artist or producer who is unable to speak directly to the people—moving the audience in some way—is not in the business for long. In America, record company execs often don't find out what is popular in clubs until they read about it in Newsweek (yet they can make any song a hit by throwing enough money at it). Jamaican producers are often label owners and sound system operators. They have always had immediate, direct feedback from their customers about every record they press. In the sixties, a producer would record all day with the best session musicians on the island. As the players headed off to their night gigs, the producer would cut the best tunes of the day onto lacquer "dub plates." In a few hours, they could audition them for the crowds, who demanded their favorites be played repeatedly throughout the night. It was only after a song became a proven hit in the dance halls that a producer would consider pressing vinyl copies for sale; he only bothered to press the records he knew would sell. If a producer wanted to take a chance on an unknown singer, or experiment with some crazy idea, all he had to risk was an hour (maybe) of studio time and the cost of a few acetates. If the song flopped, on to the next one; if it was a hit, all the better (the producer probably owned all the publishing rights in any case). This system of immediate feedback from the fans has kept the producers in touch with the record buying public. The result of this intimacy with the fans has been a vital, living body of music with a deep respect for its roots. At the same time, Reggae has an insistence that the music speak to the present.

When Jamaican producers started using multi-track recorders in the mid 1960s, they realized it was cheaper to make a new record by taking the rhythm track of an old hit and have a singer "voice" a new song on top of it. The practice of "versioning" started as a way to cut costs, but turned out to be extremely popular in Jamaica. When a new record based on a popular rhythm track gets played in the dancehall, the audience first gets a rush of recognition when they hear the track start up, followed by the seemingly contradictory pleasure of hearing a whole new song thereafter.

The people loved this, and soon dancehall selectors (DJs) were stringing together multiple songs based on the same rhythm track. These "version excursions" brought a new level of compositional complexity to the music. Each excursion was a unique combination of records and DJ jive talk created fresh every night, based on whatever got the best crowd response. In between vocal versions, the DJ would slip on the instrumental B-side (usually just labeled "version") and rap over it. It wasn't long before someone thought to do the same thing in the studio and the rap record was born. Since many of the chord progressions were the same, the easiest way to distinguish different rhythm tracks was by their basslines. These basslines became so popular in their own right that soon other producers were recording their own versions of popular rhythm tracks. As the years passed, new producers would often try to score an instant hit by recreating a popular rhythm track from years past. In the Jamaican record business popular new rhythm tracks, or riddims, appear every year (and are promptly appropriated by every producer around). However, there inevitably is a batch of re-versioned classic rhythms that also make the charts. If you listen to a Reggae radio show, purchase a new album of Reggae music, or attend a live Reggae show, you are almost guaranteed to hear new songs with basslines dating back twenty or thirty years. The tempo may be different, the style of drumming is likely to be whatever is currently popular, but the bassline remains the same, almost unchanged from when it was first recorded. A well known example of this occurred when an instrumental called "Full Up" mutated into an international hit in the early eighties—Musical Youth's "Pass the Dutchie." More recently, the rhythm from the Heptones' hit "Party Time" went straight to #1 on the US charts backing Ini Kamoze's "Here Comes the Hot Stepper." Both of these tracks originated at Coxsone Dodd's Studio 1 in the late 1960s. Most of the truly "classic" rhythms came either from Studio 1 or from Dodd's biggest rival, Duke Reid (owner of the Treasure Isle recording studio and record label).

Although the studio musicians that created these rhythms are largely unknown to the mainstream Reggae audience (in Jamaica or abroad), men such as Studio 1 keyboardist/arranger Jackie Mittoo (who wrote many of the basslines), guitarist Lynn Taitt, and bassists Jackie Jackson, Lloyd Brevett, and Leroy Sibbles helped create a musical canon that has stood the test of time. To this day, if a singer has to work with a pick-up band, all he has to say is "'Answer Rhythm' in G" and the band will know to play the bassline from Slim Smith's sixties hit "Never Let Go." While some might consider this a lack of originality, it's no more "unoriginal" than playing a 12-bar blues. The simple conventions of the musical form challenge each new performer to leave his or her own stamp on an otherwise "generic" style. Unlike the blues, Reggae produces popular new rhythms that join the canon every year. The producer or musician whose work is chosen for immortality in this fashion can only feel honored.

—Art Cohen

Art Cohen first discovered ska music when he heard Madness' "One Step Beyond" on the radio in 1979. A couple of years later, after his drummer explained to him that reggae was much, much cooler, he discovered the music of Steel Pulse, Bob Marley, and Black Uhuru. Since then, he has gone on to play guitar and bass in such Boston-based bands as Steady Earnest and Dion Knibb & the Agitators, as well as filling in with everyone from local ska-popsters Beat Soup to the legendary Skatalites. In his non-spare time, he is a computer programmer.

INTRODUCTION

The title *Reggae Bass* is actually a little misleading. Reggae is the name of a stylistic period in Jamaican popular music; however, it has become a generic term for all popular Jamaican music from the late fifties up to the present. Really, this book should be called *Jamaican Bass*.

The bass plays an important role in Jamaican music. More than just the traditional anchor, it acts as a rhythmic and melodic "hook" that defines the entire song. Bass lines are known as *riddims*—as spoken in the tongue of Jamaican English. These riddims become compositions in their own right, and are continually re-interpreted through the years. The riddims of Jamaican bass playing become standards, forming a repertoire of must-know patterns for anyone attempting the style.

SOME HISTORY

The periods of Jamaican music we will look at start around the late 1950s and continue up to the present. Until the late fifties, the predominant style of music in Jamaica was *Mento*. Basically a folk music blended from the traditions of many cultures, Mento combined instrumentation used by the African slaves brought to Jamaica with the chord structures of their European captors. There were rhythmic influences from nearby Cuba, and traces of calypso from Trinidad. Mento evolved in the late 1950s into *Ska*. The original Ska period was roughly 1955 to 1966. There have been several Ska revivals since then, one occurring from the early-mid seventies through the early eighties with the rise of the faster "English Beat" groups, and one currently taking place in the mid to late nineties with many American pop groups adapting the faster Ska groove with rock 'n' roll. The original Ska period can be broken down into two parts, the earliest of which was a product of Mento blending with the swing and R&B music that Jamaicans first heard from American soldiers stationed there.

Toward the early sixties, Ska began to develop a more pronounced Jamaican character. With a heavy accent on the upbeat, Ska is a medium tempo dance music that was popularized by deejays playing records on their portable sound systems. These sound systems were mobile discotheques that brought the music to the people. Heavy competition among the various deejays led to a boom in Ska production, each deejay procuring or producing the newest releases for their systems in an attempt to be the most popular. The upright bass was the predominant instrument of choice during the early Ska period, giving way to the electric bass later on.

In 1966, Jamaica experienced a particularly hot summer. The story has it that dancehall crowds demanded a slower groove, and so, Ska became Rock Steady. The slower tempo and the increasing use of the electric bass brought the bass line to the forefront. Somewhere around 1968, Rock Steady started a transition to the *Reggae* period. The tempo picked up slightly, but the guitar parts began to double up, playing sixteenth notes on the upbeat instead of the eighth note patterns of Rock Steady. The Reggae period continues to this day, and has many sub-styles, often dictated by changes in the drum parts and how they interact with the bass line.

The 1980s brought the advent of electronic musical instruments like drum machines, synthesizers, and sequencers. These devices found their way into Jamaican popular music and created a style known as *Dancehall*. Much of this music emphasizes keyboard bass, however many of the riddims use bass guitar with a drum machine.

THIS BOOK

Throughout this book, you will see the use of the word *riddim* to describe the bass lines presented. This is not an attempt on my part to sound more Jamaican; I'm from New York. If you are not from Jamaica, it may sound silly and be perceived as "posing" to actually call these lines "riddims," especially to a Jamaican. However, it makes it easier to distinguish when I am talking about a bass line and when I am talking about a rhythm that is part of a bass line. So, for educational purposes, I will continue to use the term "riddim" in reference to a bass line.

When multi-track recording first came to Jamaica, producers found it economical to have different singers perform over the same rhythm track. This is how certain riddims became standards. A riddim may be known by the name of its original recording, but has been used by several artists to cut new songs. The riddims of Jamaica form a fascinating lineage; tracing a bass line back through the many "versions" to its original recording is a lesson in economy and variation. This book will focus on the classic riddims of Jamaican bass from the early Ska days, through Rock Steady, into Reggae, Modern Ska, and Dancehall. As these grooves have been re-interpreted through the years, we will sometimes look at several variations of a particular riddim. All the examples will be written out in standard notation and tablature.

THE AUDIO

The audio that accompanies this book will give you the chance to play with a real Reggae rhythm section. Your band mates are Xavier Marquez on guitar, Scott Anderson on keyboards, and Carl Cherry on drums. They are present and former members of Neon Prophet, a popular Reggae band in Tucson, Arizona. Imagine how fortunate I was to find these guys here; it's a long way from Kingston! The bass tracks were performed by myself, mostly on a Precision Bass with LaBella Flatwound strings. All the examples with an audio icon next to them have a number corresponding to the track number on the audio. It is recorded in a split-mix, with the bass and drums on the left channel and the keyboard, guitar, and drums on the right. Once you feel comfortable with an example, turn off the bass track and get in the groove with the other players. Whenever possible, the true arrangement of the riddims is kept intact. In some cases, there may be a need for two guitar parts, or a piano and organ track. As this was recorded live with a four piece rhythm section, some adjustments were necessary.

ACKNOWLEGMENTS

Special thanks must go to Art Cohen; without his valuable insight and wonderful compilations, this book would have been impossible. Thanks to my family: Sonia, Irving, Lee Ellen, and Aimee Friedland, and David Taylor. Thanks to all at Hal Leonard. Thanks to Mark Keisel, Dave Flores, and everyone at Carvin; Jim Roberts, Richard Johnston, Vicki Hartung, and everyone at Bass Player Magazine; Jim Brady Recording Studios; LaBella Strings; Pam and Larry Fishman; Bob Mick; and The Bass Place in Tempe, AZ.

ABOUT THE AUTHOR

Ed Friedland is a graduate of the High School of Music and Art in New York City, and a former faculty member of Berklee College of Music, Boston College, and Arizona State University. Ed has a Masters Degree in Education from Cambridge College in Cambridge, MA. He is a contributing editor and monthly columnist for Bass Player Magazine and has authored four other books for Hal Leonard: *Building Walking Bass Lines*, *Expanding Walking Bass Lines*, *Jazz Bass*, and *Bass Improvisation*. His performance credits include Johnny Adams, Linda Hopkins, Robert Junior Lockwood, Barrence Whitfield and the Savages, Martha and the Vandellas, The Marvellettes, The Drifters, Brook Benton, Larry Coryell, Michal Urbaniak, Robben Ford, Eddie Daniels, John Stowell, Paul Horn, Mike Metheny, Illinois Jaquette, and others. He actively performs on acoustic bass, 4-, 5-, and 6-string electric basses, as well as piccolo electric bass. Ed uses Carvin basses, LaBella strings, and Fishman transducers.

PERFORMANCE TIPS

In general, Reggae bass playing is very laid back. You will see many examples that contain sixteenth-note rhythms, yet the articulation must be relaxed—almost lazy. The Reggae sixteenth note is not the same as a Fusion sixteenth note. The groove is very heavy and the downbeat must be played with conviction. This brings up an important Reggae myth to dispel: it is widely believed that a key element of Reggae bass playing is putting a rest on beat 1. If you listen to Reggae, and look through the riddims in this book, you will find that this is not the case most of the time! In the occasional riddim where the downbeat is a rest, you must still feel the downbeat. The rest of the line depends on how you feel the blank space. Reggae bass lines are a balance of note and space. Even the smallest sixteenth-note rest plays a crucial role in how the riddim grooves. When listening to Reggae, it is important to know that the skank (the piano/guitar offbeat) is counted on the "and" of each beat. This is easier to hear in Ska, but the same holds true for Rock Steady and Reggae.

Another point worth mentioning is the need for restraint. If you are coming to Reggae from a rock or jazz background, you may be accustomed to taking liberties with the bass line. Subtle (or not so subtle) variation is one of the aspects of bass playing you may enjoy. In Reggae, the riddim is it! There is little or no variation during the course of a song. You play the riddim, and that's all. The trance-inducing repetitive nature of the bass line is decidedly African in its origins (if we can momentarily forget about the Pachelbel Canon in D major!). This repetition is also present in the music of James Brown. All his tunes had set bass lines that were played without variation. Any variations in the bass line were met with a stiff fine from "The Godfather of Soul." Of course, there are riddims that evolve over a period of time; the trick is to learn how to add to a line without losing the rhythmic drive. Aston "Family Man" Barrett's work with Bob Marley is a prime example of how riddims can be more interpretive and less static.

The sound of Reggae bass is full, round, dark, and fat. This is not the place to try your Jaco Pastorious rear-pickup-on-the-Jazz-Bass sound. If you have a two pickup instrument, use both, or perhaps the front pickup alone if you can without creating hum. Many of the top Reggae bassists use Jazz Bass style instruments, though Precision style basses also sound fine. If you have a single bridge position pickup Music Man style bass, you'll need to boost the low frequencies on the active electronics and cut the treble. In the traditional Reggae mix, the bass is way up front, heavily emphasizing the 100hz–300hz range. Many of the examples in this book are deliberately written to be performed on the lower strings, in higher positions.

Playing up higher on the E and A strings produces a fuller, boomier sound. If controlled with the proper amp settings, these positions bring out the fat sound of the bass without losing definition.

If your amplifier has a graphic equalizer, start by cutting frequencies above 1K. This will darken your sound, but still leave enough mids to get articulation. Next, start to boost around 100hz. Be careful—too much of a boost combined with high volume will blow your speakers. The louder you play, the less boost you will need. Depending on your particular bass, you may need to boost the frequencies on either side of 100hz. Remember to be careful—the author assumes no responsibility for speaker repairs! An optimal speaker setup for Reggae is a cabinet with two 15" speakers, or two separate 15" units. This will give you a full, punchy sound without too much high frequency. Other configurations can be made to work. If you have one of the newer 4X10 cabinets with a built in tweeter, the first thing to do is turn off the tweeter—you won't be needing those frequencies! If you have only one cabinet, put it directly on the floor. This will enhance the lows.

TUNING

Before we start playing, let's get in tune. Here's a G note for you to tune up to.

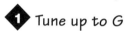 **Tune up to G**

EARLY SKA

The original Ska period ran roughly from 1959–1966. Heavily influenced by American R&B, some of the earliest Ska records were nearly identical to boogie blues. Except for the flavor of Jamaican accent in his vocals, Laurel Aitken's 1959 hit "Boogie in My Bones" could easily pass for a Big Joe Turner record. Much of the early Ska was instrumental music, performed by jazz-oriented studio musicians. The instrumentation was typical of jazz groups—horns, piano, guitar, acoustic bass, and drums. The predominant use of horns influenced Ska to be performed largely in the typical horn keys of F and B♭. The bass lines of this period were still very rooted in jazz and R&B (for the most part) quarter-note walking bass lines. As Ska progressed, rhythmic variety started to show up in the bass. It is important to note that most Reggae groups were vocal groups being backed up by the crew of studio players.

You will notice on the Ska tunes on the audio, the electric bass has a sound similar to an old upright bass. This was a deliberate attempt to capture the vibe from the original recordings. You can accomplish this effect by muting the strings close to the bridge with the edge of your palm and plucking the strings with your thumb in a downstroke motion. This will take some practice; be careful not to put too much weight on the strings as this will cut off more of the string vibration than necessary. Each particular bass has its own response and you will need to find just the right touch for your instrument. Although I have notated the tablature in the original positions that an upright bassist would play, to achieve the right sound, you may want to play these examples in a higher location on the fingerboard. The shorter, fatter string lengths help simulate the sound of an upright bass being miked.

Here is a classic early-Ska bass line using walking bass in the style of "Simmer Down."

The next line is a typical early-Ska instrumental. While the bass mostly walks, there is some rhythmic activity—a sign that bassists were starting to get away from the walking pattern and define something uniquely Jamaican. This one is in the style of "Guns of Navaronne."

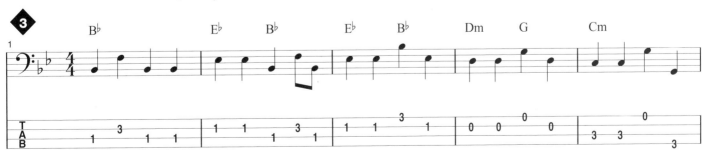

At this point, we will move on to the Rock Steady period. The early Ska approach on bass is somewhat limited to the walking bass, with some variation. If asked to interpret a song in this style, it is safe to say walking the bass line will do the job. There is a large catalog of terrific Ska recordings to be found by The Skatalites, Prince Buster, Don Drummond, a young Bob Marley with his vocal group The Wailers, Laurel Aitken, Derrick Morgan, and many others.

ROCK STEADY

Occurring between 1966 and 1968 (approximately), the Rock Steady period is where the bass really begins to take on the dominant role in Jamaican music. The slower tempo, along with the new world-wide prominence of the electric bass, became fertile ground for the development of what is now looked upon as the classic riddims of Reggae music. In this period, you will see much greater rhythmic diversity—eighth notes, sixteenth notes, and triplets, as well as quarter notes. The use of space in the bass line became very pronounced in Rock Steady. In this period, the emphasis in recording shifted more toward the vocal group, often used as a vehicle for social commentary. The practice of *versioning* or re-using pre-existing rhythm tracks had its start during the Rock Steady period. Many of the riddims you hear from later periods of Reggae were recorded in this time. This recycling process sometimes makes it hard to pinpoint a definite stylistic period for a riddim.

Here is a classic "transitional" Rock Steady riddim in the style of "Dancing Mood":

Here is a very melodic riddim in the style of "Take It Easy." Remember: the rest is as important as the notes.

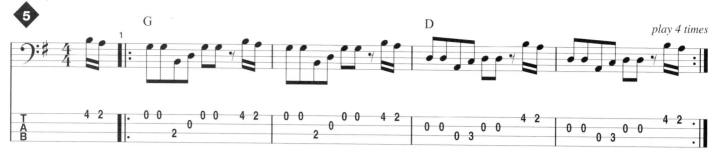

The next riddim borrows heavily from American R&B/soul, and is similar to "Girl I've Got a Date."

This riddim has a sixteenth-note figure that lays back so far, it comes very close to becoming an eighth-note triplet. This one is in the style of "Happy Go Lucky Girl."

Around 1967, an element appeared called *Rude Boy* music. The lyrics spoke to the growing number of dis-enfranchised urban youth in Kingston. This riddim, in the style of "007," is a classic example of Rude Boy music.

14

This "rudie" has an eighth rest on beat one—not as common in Reggae as you would think. It's similar to "Tougher than Tough."

The insistent pounding on the root, moving up to repeated ♭7ths creates a hypnotic effect in this riddim—in the style of "Ba Ba Boom."

*Key signature denotes B♭ Mixolydian.

The next riddim (in the style of "Carry Go Bring Home") rests on beat one and uses chord tones in eighth notes.

The heavy use of repeated sixteenth notes is a common aspect of many riddims. The following riddim (similar to "Queen Majesty") is a good example of this practice.

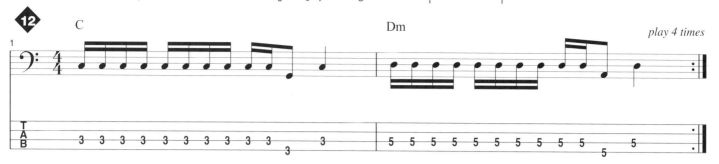

The use of the root going to the 5th with multiple repeats of the 5th is a common movement in Reggae bass. Here is an early example comparable to "Rub a Dub Style."

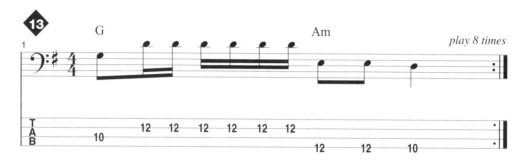

This riddim uses the same basic pattern but also goes through some chord changes. It's in the Style of "Barb Wire."

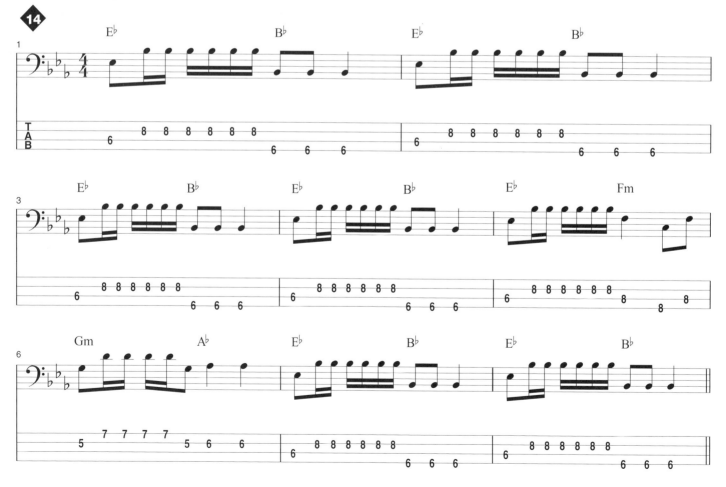

The shift between Rock Steady and Reggae is less defined than the Ska-Rock Steady transition. 1968–69 were the transitional years for this development. This example (similar to "Real Rock") of the root–5th motion rests on beat 1.

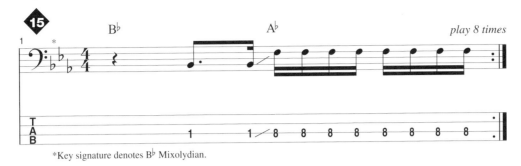

*Key signature denotes B♭ Mixolydian.

Here is another transitional riddim, this time in the style of "Love Me Forever."

This early "one drop" riddim has been reused for years. It's similar to "My Conversation."

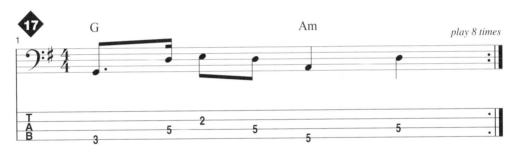

Here is another transitional riddim—in the style of "Loving Pauper."

This riddim mixes eighth and sixteenth notes. Play the sixteenths with laid back feel. This one's similar to "Kingly Character."

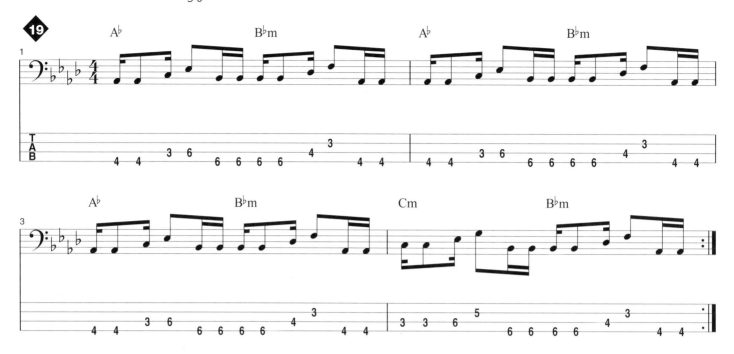

REGGAE

This is the period that gives all Jamaican popular music its name. It is a stylistic period that is seen as ongoing. In Reggae, the bass becomes an even stronger influence—anchoring the beat and giving the drummer more freedom to experiment. Many of the characteristic grooves of Reggae came from this new freedom drummers had. The "One Drop," "Rockers," "Steppers," "Lover's Rock," and "Flyers" grooves are all dictated mostly by the drummer; the bass lines for these riddims do not have specific characteristics that define each one. Many of these stylistic variations were developed from the pre-existing foundations by Reggae drummer Sly Dunbar, along with his partner in rhythm, bassist Robbie Shakespeare. Bob Marley is quoted as saying the change from Rock Steady to Reggae occurred when the guitar went from the single "skank" on the upbeat to the doubled "reggae" rhythm.

This one-measure pattern is a classic early Reggae riddim in the style of "54–46."

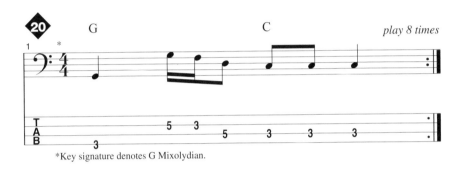

*Key signature denotes G Mixolydian.

This riddim is considered to be one of the earliest examples of the Reggae period. It's similar to "Nanny Goat."

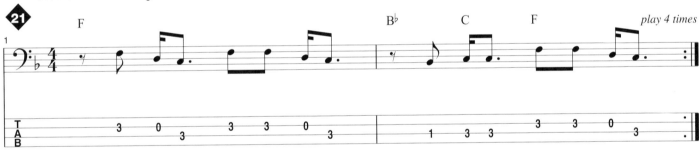

Here's another classic early Reggae line—this time in the style of "Throw Me Corn."

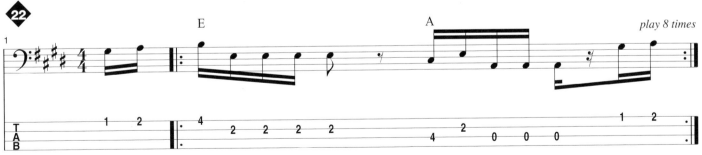

This is a variation of the riddim heard on 🔟7️⃣—a classic that gets used over and over—and is in the style of "Better Dub."

This one has a repetitive figure that moves through some changes. It's similar to "Ali Baba."

*Play through whole form twice.

Some of the early Reggae is also known as "skinhead" Reggae due to its popularity with the British youth culture of the same name. It is typified by a faster beat and a "scratchy" rhythmic feel—often in the guitar part. The next several figures are some examples of skinhead Reggae.

Here is a very active riddim. The D♭ major scale in the last two beats makes for a tricky return down to the low B♭. This one's in the style of "The Israelite."

This riddim rests on beat 1 and has a unique chromatic run. It's similar to "Shu Be Du."

Here's another example that rests on beat 1. It's similar to **11**, except the chords tones move up instead of down. This one's in the style of "Longshot Kick De Bucket."

The following riddims belong to another subgroup of the Reggae period. This period has no particular name, but is considered to be "non-Skinhead" and "pre-Roots".

This riddim rests on beat 1, has lots of space, and emphasizes the fifth of the chord structure. It's similar to the tune "Money in My Pocket."

This classic riddim has a great bouncy feel. The dead note gives it a real lift. This was one of the first riddims to turn on a lot of people worldwide on to Reggae music. It's done in the style of "The Harder They Come."

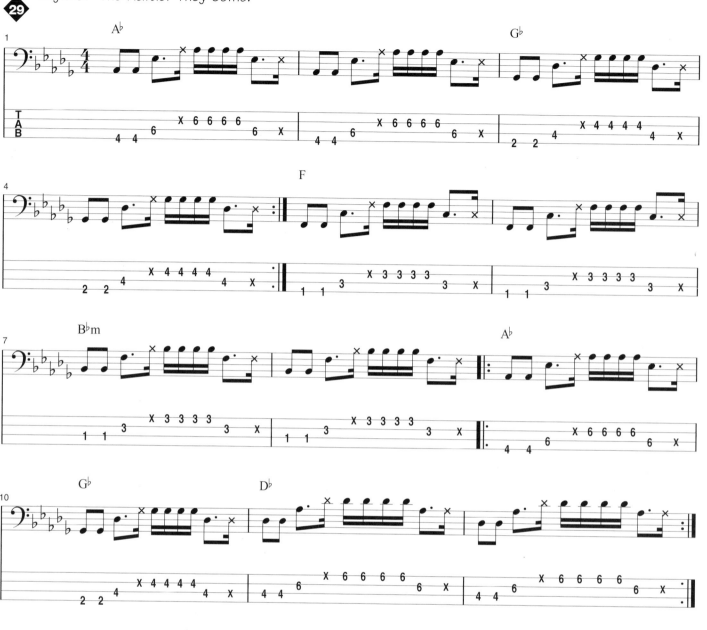

Notice how the space in this one allows the groove to happen—similar to "S.90 Skank."

Here is a classic riddim with a very cool variation in the second half. This one's done in the style of "Skylarking."

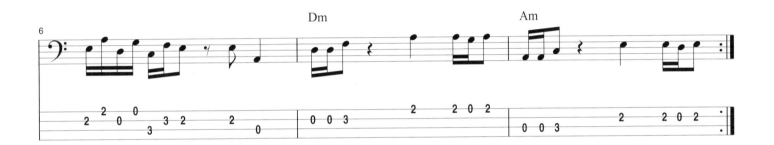

ROOTS REGGAE

Abig development in Reggae was the influence of the Rastafarian religion in Jamaica. Outwardly, the dreadlocked hair and use of marijuana as a sacred ritual are elements of the Rasta faith that people pick up on. On a deeper level, the religion acknowledges the African heritage of Jamaica's black population, and a belief that they are destined to return one day to Africa, their spiritual home. The connection between Rastafarianism and Reggae music created the "Roots" period. The lyrical content is mostly oriented toward cultural consciousness raising, and the chord structures started to emphasize more minor sounds. While many groups are responsible for the rise of the Roots movement, Bob Marley is recognized as the most prominent artist of this period.

Here is an early example of Roots Reggae. It's performed in the style of "Satta Massa Gana."

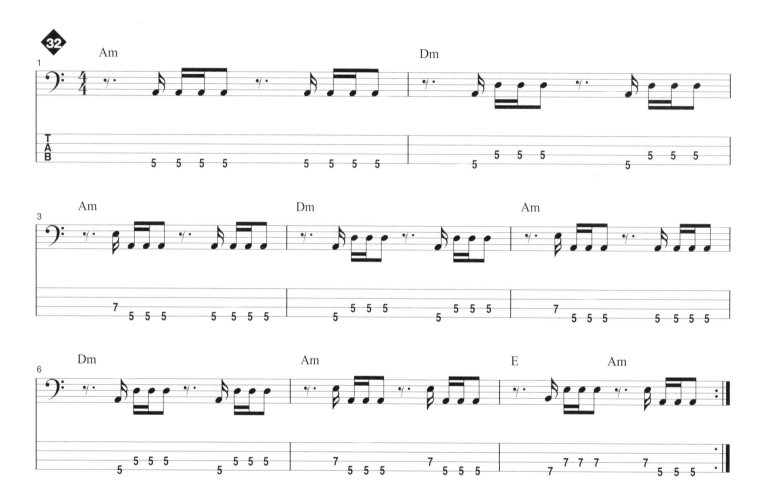

This one-measure pattern is also pure Roots, and is in the style of "Marcus Garvey."

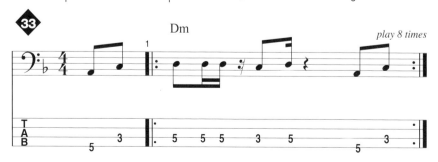

24

The small slide up to G in this one is a nice effect. This riddim is similar to "War Inna Babylon."

This riddim echoes some R&B influences, and is in the style of "Two 7's Clash."

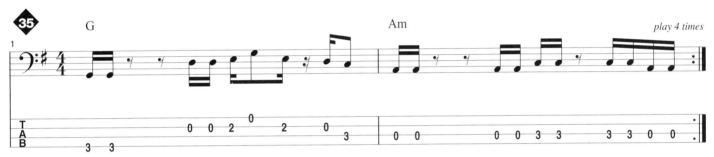

This two-part riddim has a unique slide in measure 4. The B section uses a triplet starting on the ♭3rd of the C minor chord to create some rhythmic and melodic tension. This one is in the style of "Get Up Stand Up."

*Play through entire form twice.

Section A of this riddim is a repeating four-measure phrase with lots of space. The B section uses the octave–5th–root pattern in a descending "rake" fashion. This track is similar to "I Shot the Sheriff."

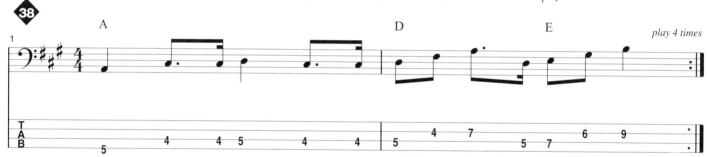

Here is a relaxed line that uses major triads (in the style of "Stir it Up").

Here is a shuffle-type riddim. The straight eighth notes should also be interpreted with a triplet feel. This one's similar to "Jammin'."

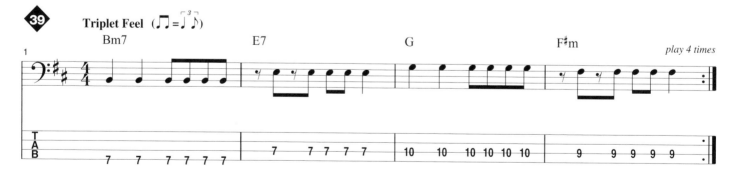

DUB

Dub is a stylistic period of Reggae that borrowed heavily on the riddims of the past. As in most Reggae, riddims were "versioned" for years after their initial release. Dub came into play as studio technology improved, allowing more adventurous re-mixes of old classics to be created. These dubs were used largely as platforms for DJs to rap or "toast" to in the dance halls. I have chosen not to include any Dub riddims, as they are mostly re-mixes of pre-existing lines. If there is a Dub "style" to be learned, it would be to develop a feeling for when the various instruments lay out. Dub mixes generally feature the appearance and disappearance of the various instruments at frequent intervals. While there is no set pattern for these occurrences, it is possible to create a Dub mix on a live gig by selectively laying out when the feeling is right.

MODERN SKA

In the late 1970s and early 1980s, Ska made its first big comeback. A movement started in England where Jamaican ex-patriots and English punk rockers joined forces. This unlikely blend created a mix of Punk energy and Ska sophistication. Groups like The Specials, The Selector, The Beat, and UB40 took old Ska classics, sped them up, and created a movement sometimes called "Two-Tone"—named after an English record label. Another goal of the Two-Tone movement was to promote racial harmony among the working class white and black youth of the UK. Many of the bands were racially mixed, and the appeal of the music was broad. We are once again in the midst of another Ska revival in the United States. Many young bands have re-discovered the Ska classics, some through the records of the English Ska movement, and all eventually finding their way back to the recordings of The Skatalites and Don Drummond.

Here is a high energy line from the English Ska period in the style of "On My Radio."

This is a fast Ska rendition of a Motown classic. It's similar to "Tears of a Clown."

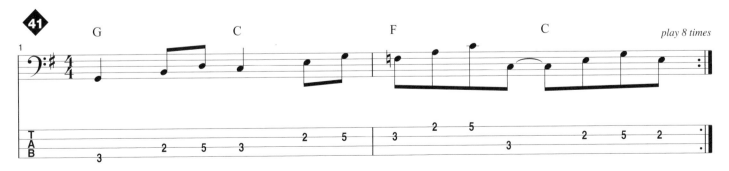

DANCEHALL

The dancehall has always played an important role in the development of Jamaican music. Before cheap transistor radios were readily available, the sound system and dancehall were the ways Jamaicans heard the new hits. In the early 1980s, Reggae became conspicuously dance-oriented. Many of the widely accepted conventions of Rap, House Music, and Techno had their start in the creative pressure cooker of Jamaican recording studios. Dancehall style also borrowed heavily from American music, and paralleled the development of mechanized record production with drum machines and synthesizers. The influx of cheap synthesizers from Japan had a big impact on how music was produced in Jamaica. Indeed, some classic Dancehall riddims were actually pre-set bass and drum patterns created by a synthesizer programmer in Japan! Many of the riddims of "Digital" Reggae are played on keyboards, yet are still important for the reggae bassist to know.

This is an early example of Dancehall style, played in the style of "Night Nurse."

This riddim is another non-digital bass line, and is similar to "Mad over Me."

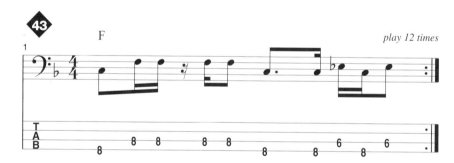

This riddim is very similar to the previous example. It's done in the style of "Tusheng Peng."

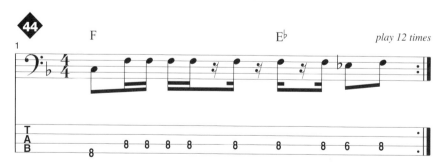

This "digital" riddim was a pre-set pattern from an inexpensive Casio keyboard. Remarkably, it became one of the most versioned riddims of Dancehall style. The following figure is similar to "Under Me Sleng Teng."

This is a unique riddim. It has more of a Latin clave-based feel than most Reggae. It is similar to the tune "Punnany."

While not a pre-set, this riddim was originally played on the auto-bass buttons found on the aforementioned Casio. It is possible to simulate this sound by using an octave divider without the original sound of the bass blended in. Play the line up an octave, and let the foot pedal drop it down with the synthesized effect. This one is in the style of "Tempo."

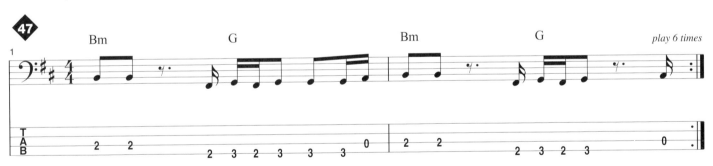

REGGAE SOURCES

While compiling this book, I found several great resources for Reggae music and information. A must-have CD compilation is *Tougher Than Tough, The Story of Jamaican Music,* on Island Records. The liner notes are very informative, and the chronological order of the recordings is very useful. A terrific book on Reggae is *Reggae, The Rough Guide,* by Steve Barrow and Peter Dalton, published by Penguin Books. This is a very comprehensive work, detailing the history and development of Jamaican popular music and its artists. It has over 1,000 recommendations for CDs and records.

If you have internet access, you're in luck; there are many great sources on-line for Reggae music. Go to *http://www.geocities.com/SiliconValley/Heights/2597/* to find "The Jamaican Riddim Directory." This site has soundfiles of many classic riddims broken into various categories. Check out http://www.niceup.com/ where you'll find the "Jammin' Reggae Archives"—a collection of information and Web links to Reggae music. At *http://www.webcity.co.jp/info/maeda/riddim01.html* you'll find "Never Grow Old," an extensive listing compiled by Keita Maeda of Reggae riddims and their various versions. This list proved very helpful in cross referencing many of the riddims in this book. Of course you can check out *www.ziplink.net/~upsetter/ska/calendar.html* put up by Art Cohen. This is the National Ska and Reggae calendar with tour information and local show listings for the entire United States. There is a lot of Reggae out there on the Web. Once you start searching, you can find more information than you can imagine.

I hope you have found this compilation of Reggae bass lines helpful and fun.

BASS NOTATION LEGEND

Bass music can be notated two different ways: on a *musical staff*, and in *tablature*.

THE MUSICAL STAFF shows pitches and rhythms and is divided by bar lines into measures. Pitches are named after the first seven letters of the alphabet.

TABLATURE graphically represents the bass fingerboard. Each horizontal line represents a string, and each number represents a fret.

3rd string, open   2nd string, 2nd fret   1st & 2nd strings open, played together

HAMMER-ON: Strike the first (lower) note with one finger, then sound the higher note (on the same string) with another finger by fretting it without picking.

PULL-OFF: Place both fingers on the notes to be sounded. Strike the first note and without picking, pull the finger off to sound the second (lower) note.

LEGATO SLIDE: Strike the first note and then slide the same fret-hand finger up or down to the second note. The second note is not struck.

SHIFT SLIDE: Same as legato slide, except the second note is struck.

TRILL: Very rapidly alternate between the notes indicated by continuously hammering on and pulling off.

TREMOLO PICKING: The note is picked as rapidly and continuously as possible.

VIBRATO: The string is vibrated by rapidly bending and releasing the note with the fretting hand.

SHAKE: Using one finger, rapidly alternate between two notes on one string by sliding either a half-step above or below.

NATURAL HARMONIC: Strike the note while the fret hand lightly touches the string directly over the fret indicated.

MUFFLED STRINGS: A percussive sound is produced by laying the fret hand across the string(s) without depressing them and striking them with the pick hand.

BEND: Strike the note and bend up the interval shown.

BEND AND RELEASE: Strike the note and bend up as indicated, then release back to the original note. Only the first note is struck.

RIGHT-HAND TAP: Hammer ("tap") the fret indicated with the "pick-hand" index or middle finger and pull off to the note fretted by the fret hand.

LEFT-HAND TAP: Hammer ("tap") the fret indicated with the "fret-hand" index or middle finger.

SLAP: Strike ("slap") string with right-hand thumb.

POP: Snap ("pop") string with right-hand index or middle finger.

ADDITIONAL MUSICAL DEFINITIONS

 (accent) • Accentuate note (play it louder)

(accent) • Accentuate note with great intensity

(staccato) • Play the note short

• Downstroke

V • Upstroke

D.S. al Coda • Go back to the sign (𝄋), then play until the measure marked "***To Coda***," then skip to the section labelled "***Coda***."

D.C. al Fine • Go back to the beginning of the song and play until the measure marked "***Fine***" (end).

Bass Fig. • Label used to recall a recurring pattern.

Fill • Label used to identify a brief pattern which is to be inserted into the arrangement.

tacet • Instrument is silent (drops out).

 • Repeat measures between signs.

 • When a repeated section has different endings, play the first ending only the first time and the second ending only the second time.

NOTE: Tablature numbers in parentheses mean:
1. The note is being sustained over a system (note in standard notation is tied), or
2. The note is sustained, but a new articulation (such as a hammer-on, pull-off, slide or vibrato begins, or
3. The note is a barely audible "ghost" note (note in standard notation is also in parentheses).

BASS BUILDERS

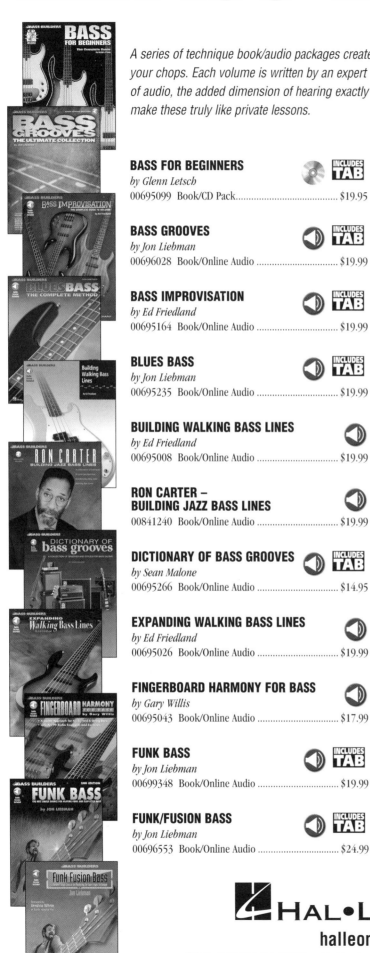

A series of technique book/audio packages created for the purposeful building and development of your chops. Each volume is written by an expert in that particular technique. And with the inclusion of audio, the added dimension of hearing exactly how to play particular grooves and techniques make these truly like private lessons.

BASS FOR BEGINNERS
by Glenn Letsch
00695099 Book/CD Pack.........................$19.95

BASS GROOVES
by Jon Liebman
00696028 Book/Online Audio $19.99

BASS IMPROVISATION
by Ed Friedland
00695164 Book/Online Audio $19.99

BLUES BASS
by Jon Liebman
00695235 Book/Online Audio $19.99

BUILDING WALKING BASS LINES
by Ed Friedland
00695008 Book/Online Audio $19.99

RON CARTER – BUILDING JAZZ BASS LINES
00841240 Book/Online Audio $19.99

DICTIONARY OF BASS GROOVES
by Sean Malone
00695266 Book/Online Audio $14.95

EXPANDING WALKING BASS LINES
by Ed Friedland
00695026 Book/Online Audio $19.99

FINGERBOARD HARMONY FOR BASS
by Gary Willis
00695043 Book/Online Audio $17.99

FUNK BASS
by Jon Liebman
00699348 Book/Online Audio $19.99

FUNK/FUSION BASS
by Jon Liebman
00696553 Book/Online Audio $24.99

HIP-HOP BASS
by Josquin des Prés
00695589 Book/Online Audio $15.99

JAZZ BASS
by Ed Friedland
00695084 Book/Online Audio $17.99

JERRY JEMMOTT – BLUES AND RHYTHM & BLUES BASS TECHNIQUE
00695176 Book/CD Pack.........................$24.99

JUMP 'N' BLUES BASS
by Keith Rosier
00695292 Book/Online Audio $17.99

THE LOST ART OF COUNTRY BASS
by Keith Rosier
00695107 Book/Online Audio $19.99

PENTATONIC SCALES FOR BASS
by Ed Friedland
00696224 Book/Online Audio $19.99

REGGAE BASS
by Ed Friedland
00695163 Book/Online Audio $16.99

'70S FUNK & DISCO BASS
by Josquin des Prés
00695614 Book/Online Audio $16.99

SIMPLIFIED SIGHT-READING FOR BASS
by Josquin des Prés
00695085 Book/Online Audio $17.99

6-STRING BASSICS
by David Gross
00695221 Book/Online Audio $14.99

HAL•LEONARD®

halleonard.com

Prices, contents and availability subject to change without notice; All prices are listed in U.S. funds